Catching Waves

A BOARD, A PIG, AND HOW A LITTLE GIRL BECAME A WAKESURF CHAMPION

WRITTEN AND ILLUSTRATED BY DAWN MARIE HOOKS

PAPER MOON
PUBLICATIONS

Raleigh was born with a surfboard at her feet. Not really, of course, but it sure seemed that way. She was only five when she caught her first wave during a family trip to the beach.

Surf Crash Splash

She shredded.

She ripped.

She surfed.

"I want to be a surfer girl," she decided.

She took trips to the coast, but it wasn't enough. At the end of every trip, she put away her surfboard and her dream. She lived in central Texas—too far from the waves to be a surfer girl.

Until one day when Raleigh was eight...

Dad whisked her away to the nearby lake.

How was she supposed to surf on a lake?

They had a plan. Raleigh would
surf the wake behind a boat.

Raleigh slid into the water. Gripping the tow rope's
handle, she planted her feet on her surfboard. Dad
drove the boat forward. The rope pulled.

Crash She tried again.

 *Splash* Over and over.

Finally, as the boat surged forward,
Raleigh popped to standing.

Surf

Crash

Splash

Over and over, until she was gliding on the water,
gripping the rope's handle. It wasn't quite like surfing
(because the rope was pulling her), but it was fun.

One day, when
Raleigh was riding,
she tossed the rope.

She shifted her body,
pressed her toes, and
maneuvered her board
until she could stay in the
sweet spot (the part of
the wake that pushes like
an ocean wave), until...

no rope
no problem.

By the time she
was nine, she
could wakesurf
for hours.
She surfed.
She carved.
She slashed.

Those who saw her shook their heads in amazement.

"She's a natural," they said.

So, Raleigh entered her first competition.

Would the wake be big enough?

Would the boat take off too fast?

Could she do her tricks on a short course?

She breathed deeply, reminding herself that

this was just another chance to wakesurf.

When it was her turn, she ripped from the start buoy,

down the course, and back—one minute each way.

Fans watched. Judges scored every move.

Raleigh placed second in the women's open. It was awesome!

Wakesurfing became her passion.

2ⁿᵈ Place   1ˢᵗ Place   3ʳᵈ Place

Women's Open

Yet the more Raleigh surfed, the more she was left out with friends. She missed playdates, sleepovers, and school events.

But she loved wakesurfing...

Still, Raleigh had another desire. She wanted a pet micro mini pig. She had begged and pleaded.

Mom and Dad *always* said,

"No."

Then, Raleigh had an idea:

What if she became a professional and placed in the World Wake Surfing Championship, the biggest wakesurf competition in the world? Then could she have a pig?

"Sure," Dad said, thinking it was impossible. Raleigh had never competed as a pro. No child had. How could she possibly place in the world championship?

Raleigh hurried through homework.

She skipped morning cartoons.

Not even winter stopped her. Oh, it was cold, even in a wetsuit, but that didn't chill the thrill inside her. She surfed until her toes were numb.

She practiced until wakesurfing was as easy as eating sushi, her favorite food.

At ten, Raleigh flew to California for her first professional competition. Could she hold her own against the best adults?

Raleigh waited, watching the other wakesurfers. Then, she shredded. She ripped. She surfed.

She finished in third place, earning her spot as a pro.

It was awesome!

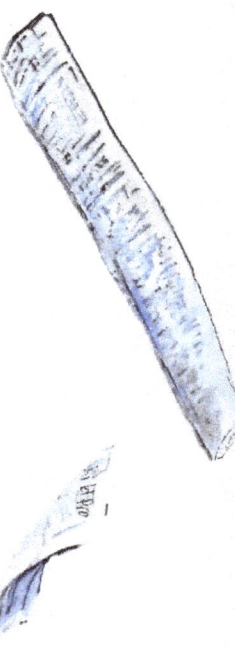

Sponsors sent free gear.

Reporters interviewed her.

Photographers snapped pictures.

Fans begged for autographs.

She was in newspapers,

magazines, and videos—

the only kid pro wakesurfer.

Raleigh kept practicing and

claiming trophies. It seemed like

nothing could hold her back

until ...

Raleigh traveled to Minnesota for the last major competition before the world championship. She shredded. She ripped. She surfed.

But, for the first time, Raleigh went home empty-handed. Her best surfing hadn't scored well. It did not seem fair.

Would she quit?

Not a chance. She wanted to make it to Worlds, and she wanted a pet pig. Raleigh practiced and practiced. She surfed and surfed.

Sometimes, her legs were too stiff.

Crash

Her body twisted too far.

Wipeout

She tried a new trick and fell every single time.

Surf   Splash   Crash

Over and over, until her body ached, and she could barely breathe.

Until she slashed
so forcefully, the
water sprayed
like a fountain.

She jumped
so high, she
felt like she
was flying.

She spun so
gracefully, she
looked like a
ballerina.

Finally, it was time. Raleigh flew to Arizona for the three-day World Wake Surfing Championship. She groaned when she saw the professionals. They were so much older and so much more experienced than her.

"*This is all I've wanted to do. This is the biggest competition there is for wakesurfing,*" Raleigh thought.

Plus, she wanted a pig.

Judges boarded the boat.

Photographers prepared their cameras.

Raleigh waxed her board.

When it was her turn, Raleigh shredded.

Would she move on to the semi-finals,

or would this be it?

Raleigh didn't think she'd done well

enough.

Mom saw the scores.

"YOU MADE IT!"

"Cool. I get to surf again," Raleigh said.

On day two, Raleigh ripped. Again, she waited for the results.

"Raleigh, you made it to finals," said Mom.

It was unreal.
It was unheard of.
It was awesome!
No kid had ever competed as a pro, and no kid had ever competed in the world championship finals.

On the final day of the world championship, Raleigh's
stomach felt like a pinball machine.

She slid into the water with her board,

reached for the rope,

and **puked**—right there in the water.

At least her stomach wasn't aching anymore.

She focused. She surfed. She threw in all her best tricks.

Would it be enough?

Finally, the other wakesurfers finished, and the scores were computed. Everyone gathered, their eyes on the announcer.

"Rebekah Ort, third place."

Raleigh's heart dropped. Deep down, she dared to hope that she'd made second.

"Second place, Ashley Kidd."

Her eyes filled with tears as she clapped for the others.

"First place, Pro Women's World Champion is none other than ten-year-old, Raleigh Hager!"

The crowd exploded with cheers.
Dad and Mom burst into tears.

"Whaaaat?" Raleigh beamed. "I get my pig!"

Raleigh earned the title of Women's Pro World Wakesurf Champion. She earned the nickname, "The Phenom" because she was phenomenal, and she earned a pet pig she named Fergus.

Fergus did not learn to wakesurf. He pooped when he went into the water. And that's worse than puking.

AUTOHOR NOTES

Raleigh Hager and her parents at the 2012 World Wake Surfing Championship, Photos courtesy of JB Hager

More About Raleigh: In 2012, ten-year-old Raleigh Hager became the youngest person to compete as a professional and the youngest professional World Wake Surfing Champion. She also won the next world championship in 2013 when she was eleven years old. If you are out on Lake Austin in Texas, you might see Raleigh shredding behind a boat or giving a lesson to the next generation of wakesurfers. You might even see her compete nearby. Fergus, Raleigh's micro mini pig, grew to be about fifty pounds.

Writing Her Story: I hope Raleigh's story inspires you as much as it inspired me. I first watched Raleigh compete in 2014 when she was twelve. After hearing tidbits of her story, I interviewed Raleigh and her family. The first phone interview motivated me to learn more about wakesurfing and competition. I signed up for my first wakesurfing lesson and my first competition, where I met Raleigh and her parents in person. Soon, I was competing in the masters division (age 35+) and eventually became the 2019

World Champion in my division. My experiences and friendships in the sport gave me abundant enthusiasm and appreciation as I worked on this book. I want to thank those who teach lessons, organize and sponsor events, shape boards, support competitors, and especially those who cheer for each other. I also want to thank Raleigh Hager and her parents for being so open and supportive of this book.

Wakesurfing: Every year, the athletes develop new tricks as the boards, boats, and waves improve. It's thrilling to see the progression of wakesurfing over the years and the amazing things the young wakesurfers do on their boards!

Raleigh Hager in 2024, Photos courtesy of JB Hager

GLOSSARY

Buoy – a marker that floats in the water. In wakesurf competitions, it is usually bright orange and marks the beginning and the end of the course.

Carve – to surf up and down the wave or wake

Division – the category of the wakesurfer during competitions, the group they compete against

Professional or *Pro* – the highest level of competing in wakesurfing

Rip or *Shred* – to surf aggressively

Slash – to sharply turn the surfboard on the wave so it splashes water

Tow rope – the rope which is attached to the boat on one end and a handle on the other end. The wakesurfer holds the handle and is pulled to standing as the boat moves forward.

Wake – the wave that the boat makes when it is moving. In wakesurfing, the boat is set so the wake/wave is back behind one side of the boat.

Wakesurf or *Wake surf* – surfing the wake formed behind a boat

HIGHLIGHTS FROM RALEIGH'S FIRST YEARS OF COMPETITION

Age 9

- October 2011, Barrel Boss Wake Surf Competition (Lake Austin, TX), Junior 3rd place, Women's Open 2nd place
- October 2011, Waketoberfest Wakesurf Contest (Canyon Lake, TX), Women's Open 1st place

Age 10

- May 2012, West Coast Wakesurf Open (Camp Far West, CA), Women's Pro Surf 3rd place
- July 2012, USA National Wake Surf Championship (Orlando, Fl), Women's Pro Surf 3rd place
- August 2012, 10K Lakes Wakesurf Open (Minneapolis, MN), Women's Pro Surf
- September 2012, World Wake Surfing Championship (Parker, AZ), Women's Pro Surf 1st place

Age 11

- April 2013, Mexico Wakesurf Championship (Loreto, Mexico), Women's Pro Surf 1st place
- May 2013, Arizona Wake Surf Championship (Phoenix, AZ), Women's Pro Surf 1st place
- May 2013, West Coast Wakesurf Open (Sacramento, CA), Women's Pro Surf 1st place
- May 2013, Swiss Wake Surf Championship (Zurich, Switzerland), Women's Pro Surf 1st place
- August 2013, 10K Lakes Wakesurf Open (Minneapolis, MN), Women's Pro Surf 1st place
- August 2013, USA National Wake Surf Championship (Callaway Gardens, GA), Women's Pro Surf 1st place
- August 2013, Texas Surf Showdown (Ft. Worth, TX), Women's Pro Surf 2nd place
- September 2013, World Wake Surfing Championship (Las Vegas, AZ), Women's Pro Surf 1st place

*For my husband, Michael Hooks, who
introduced me to wakesurfing and
encourages me in my many endeavors.*

Published in the United States by Paper Moon Publications.

Library of Congress Control Number: 2024941928

ISBN-13: 979-8-9906660-1-6 - Hardcover
ISBN-13: 979-8-9906660-0-9 - Paperback

The illustrations in this book were created using pencil, ink, watercolor, and gouache.
Visit Dawn Marie Hooks at www.dawnmariehooks.com
for more books and activity guides.

www.ingramcontent.com/pod-product-compliance
Lightning Source LLC
Chambersburg PA
CBHW041156120626
46547CB00020B/3240